ATTERRANDO

ATTERRANDO

Carmela Delia Lanza

Epigraph Books
Rhinebeck, New York

Paperback ISBN 978-1-960090-66-9

Contact the publisher for Library of Congress Control Number

Book Design by Colin Rolfe

Epigraph Books
22 East Market Street, Suite 304
Rhinebeck, New York 12572
(845) 876-4861
epigraphps.com

ATTERRANDO: landing; knocking down; burying the dead; bending to the ground.

"*atterrando l'occhio e l'muso*"
"bending eye and muzzle to the ground."
DANTE, *PURGATORIO III*, LINE 81

"I got lonely because I was going extinct
from giving and giving and giving."
JENNIFER MARTELLI, *"PANIS, PANIS, ANGELICUS: A CENTO"*

Dedicated to all my ancestors who brought me here . . .

Acknowledgments

Thanks to the editors of the following publications where the following poems were first published:

Bloodroot Literary Magazine: "*La Vergine* (Madison, South Dakota)"

BorderSenses: "Walking into The Mouth"

The Blue Collar Review: Journal of Progressive Working Class Literature: "To Burn or Bury Them"

Chantwood Magazine: "Nino's Mother" and "Saturna Finally Speaks"

Comparative Woman (LSU): "Blood Moon," "Continental Divide(s)" and "Seven Mothers"

Feile-Festa: "Cry Baby"

Imagination & Place: An Anthology: "Making Light, Crownpoint, New Mexico"

Looking Back to Place: An Anthology: "Confession"

Modern Language Studies: "In the Long Island Sound with My Father" and "Tarot and an Italian American Girl on Long Island"

Ovunque Siamo: "Owning Venice for Awhile" and "Remembering What I Saw: A Glosa"

Red Mesa Review: "Language in My Mouth"

Southwestern Women: New Voices: "Grace"

Voices in Italian Americana: "No One Knows Much About Us" and "*E Lucevan Le Stelle* in Dawson, New Mexico, 1912"

Wordrunner eChapbooks: "Memento" (earlier version)

The following poems appeared in the chapbook, *So Rough A Messenger*, Finishing Line Press, 2014:
"Wall Cloud (Driving from New Mexico to South Dakota)"
"*La Vergine* (Madison, South Dakota)"
"This Desert"
"Walking to El Santuario de Chimayó, New Mexico"
"Making Light, Crownpoint, New Mexico"
"Confession"
"The Mother and The Seeds"
"Grace"

The following poems appeared in the chapbook, *Long Island Girl*, Malafemmina Press, 1992:
"Una Storia"
"Grandma Rinaldi"

Contents

PART ONE

la tammurriata . . .

" . . . The source of poetry that
seeing the clock stopped, says,
The clock has stopped

that ticked yesterday so well?
and hears the sound of lakewater
splashing—that is now stone."

WILLIAM CARLOS WILLIAMS, "THESE"

La Via Del Dolore (The Way of Pain)

I lift my old body to get a glass of water
walking in the dark, in my small house
in the middle of the night,
shadows of objects and people
and soon to disappear objects and people:
to suspire   *sospirare*

It starts with a journey and water must be involved,
another kind of birthing but this time
she cannot turn to her *mama* or *cognate* for answers.
No one knows what will happen and with that
she goes on the ship with two children;
there is no bread in the desert of ocean,
only bruises and prayers that existed
as long as the sounds coming out of her mouth,
just like the wind blowing across the graves now
in Dawson, New Mexico.
Names fading away from sun and wind and
the loss of language, body, and place.
Everything is swallowed in this place.

There was a town,
"We had everything there.
The schools were some of the best
we ever had.
The Phelps Dodge Corp. had the big store.
It had everything and they would give the miners script
so they could buy material from payday to payday . . .
when payday came around,
they collected what they owed them and
sometimes the miners were left with nothing." *

"The first time I step foot on this ground, God should have
knocked me down dead . . ."
words wandering through that now empty room,
a room that was once my entire world, a place I was able to breathe
and look out the window at the old tree that always seemed to lean
toward our house,
even when my sister was in there with me,
two girls crammed in, not quite like in the bottom of a ship
but almost, hot, airless July nights, barely a breeze and always
the sound of a mosquito somewhere,
cold, icy mornings having to touch the cracked formica floor
running to the bathroom, knowing there would not be
any hot water for at least an hour,
even then it was still my place,
the place I had dreams of Emily Dickinson's grave
or watching the wet leaves outside, I knew this
was just the beginning of something,
and now there are only words scattering through me,
not quite remembering my mother's voice when she used to say that,
sometimes she said it with a small smile,
other times in anger,
and now nothing but wind.

"A MINING TRAGEDY.
The explosion
in the
Stag Canon mine,
at Dawson, New Mexico,
by which nearly
three hundred miners
lost their lives,
was one of those
unexplained and
apparently unavoidable
tragedies
of which

the history
of mining
is full.

The mine
was considered
a model
of mining engineering,
and every means
had been taken
to secure
the safety
of the miners
at work in it,
yet an explosion
caused
perhaps
by the prevalence of coal dust,
or perhaps
by the ignition of fire damp,
wrecked
the entrances,
filled
the mine
with gas and shut up
hundreds of men
in a living tomb.
The one redeeming
feature of the
tragedy
was the courage
shown by the rescue parties,
several of whom
freely gave up
their own lives
in the desperate
effort to reach

and save
the imprisoned men." **

"More than a day has passed and yet the people
on whom the dreadful blow has fallen do not understand.
They cannot as a body grasp the horror,
its fullness, and quiet, stunned.
Only now and then is heard the keen wail
of a stricken woman as the body
at the pit mouth is identified." ***

---

* "Remembering the Dawson Mining Disaster, 100 Years Later" Tom Sharpe, *The New Mexican*, Oct. 19th, 2013

** "The Week in Review." *The Journal of Education*, Vol. 78, No. 17 (1953) (November 6, 1913), p. 450.

*** Raton Range, 1913.

Not My *'Good Old U.S.A.'*

I walk along the spine of the mesa
where nothing feels like home.
Somewhere in the mouth of a cave
I feel my mother's breath as
she talks about her little village,
San Giorgio del Sannio,
la chiesa, la fontana, the church, the fountain,
all I can hear is my mother laughing
with her friends,
maybe that is all
she wants me to hear.
There seems to be so much dancing
and talking and it seems no one is wondering
"where should I go" or "where do I belong"
she saves that for later,
after the journey,
after the choices that are really commands;
now there is a sense of entrapment,
of loss, of resignation
of

"The Good Old U.S.A."

An Italian miner, who formerly resided in Dawson
for a number of years
and who recently returned from the old country,
*says that Dawson looks like home to him.**

of walking away,
of forgetting the smell of your mother's neck,
of believing what was there was no good,
what was ahead of you had some promise,

a dream, a future, a reason,
an answer,
motion
getting ahead,
forgetting,
denying,
of what,
of

He represents conditions as deplorable
in his former home district
and with little hope of improvement
*for years to come.**

She did not talk about the bombs
or whatever starving she saw and felt,
she did not talk about the *Americani*
and what they wanted or what they joked about.
I heard her talking to my uncle about the bombs,
and when I walked in the kitchen,
they stopped.
My uncle was making a fruit salad,
he said they did not need to talk about that anymore.
It was about work, having work, looking for work,
not finding work

For the laborer, there is little, if any work,
while prices for the common necessities of life
*are almost prohibitive.**

The refrigerator always full,
the small freezer next to it always full,
piles of newspapers on the chair by the radiator,
piles of newspapers on the washing machine,
fruit and walnuts and bags of cookies and crackers,

Having a fair supply of American money,

*he and his family did not suffer**

I look at Italian sewing machines on Ebay for hours
but I don't know how to sew.
There is my hunger: I want to be surrounded
so I don't feel like I am drowning or
that I am lost.

as the Italian lira, normally worth about 20 cents
is now worth 4 cents in American money.
*One American dollar was worth 25 liras**

I count the days until my next paycheck.

but with a pair of shoes costing 250 liras
*and all living costs in proportion**

My mother wore plastic shoes
and every night her feet were red and swollen.
They were shoes that were synthetic leather,
never softening, never cradling her feet;
her slippers were hard and tight;
she never seemed to like standing or walking.
She described the shoes she wore in Italy,
the ones made for her;
I will not wear synthetic leather.
Sometimes I look at my feet and cry,
they are also swollen and wide,
I cannot hide where I am from,
where we all were from.

*His fare from Italy home cost him 7,000 lira.**

How did my grandmother pay for all of her children?
How long did she patiently save the money?
How did she know "this is right."?
Did anyone tell her years later,

sitting in her kitchen in Harrison, New York,
"You were right, Ma. You did the right thing."
Did she tell herself, "This is not the place."
She never talked about this place,
never talked about the beauties of the United States,
never talked about how grateful she was.
She created her own *pease*, her own village
in this place and her children and grand-children would visit.
She moved slowly from the kitchen to the living room
to her bedroom, and that was her circle,
speaking *Napolitana* with my mother,
she did not cry
even when she talked about her sisters
back in their village, *San Giorgio del Sannio*,
only my mother cried about what they experienced at home
and what they were experiencing in this place.

Just what obstacles the new restrictions on immigration
will present to the bringing back
of his family
to America
is now
*his greatest concern.**

* "The Good Old U.S.A." *The Dawson News*, March 17, 1921.

No One Knows Much About Us

Giovanina Antonelli (1910-1911)

Christine Antonelli (1916-1916)

buried at Dawson Cemetery, Dawson, New Mexico

We play in the garden of the dead,
my sister and I,
I was first and then her;
La Befana the Beautiful visited each of us,
wiping our foreheads,
spitting on our hands and feet,
knowing what would be
before we said our first word.

but I remember saying Mama,
mamamama,
mamamamamama
over and over
my song

She knew we would not share any secrets,
whispering at night,
too small to prepare for battles
except the only one that mattered,
the one that took first me and then my sister.
I wanted to ask La Befana,
"What does it mean to have a sister?"
But she would have probably said,
"Ssh, piccola, non ti preoccupare,
piccola, non piangere."

I never saw the town
only smelled it, the smoke and dirt

and something else that I would never understand.
I sat in a dark cave,
watching my mother cry for some place
so far away.

When my sister arrived I was still there waiting
but no one saw me.
Only La Befana and I
holding hands,
waiting for my sister to say one word
but she never did.
Silence was her song as she watched me
approach with my sword.
She was looking in the mirror for a second,
a slice of light caught her eyes,
the gold necklace she was wearing
glimmering for a moment,
and that was all it took for me,
a wound that would never heal.
Maybe others would hold on to olive oil or garlic
or a rag of linen used to wrap up
what was left of a life,
soon forgotten on a heap of trash
and here we are,
rising from our shallow graves,
we do not ask for protection
as we battle it out every day
in the garden,
we are *i benandanti* of this place,
telling our story to no one.

To Burn or Bury Them

In this city,
the dead are buried,
the quiet is there as before,
whatever coins or rings are left behind,
somewhere deep in the clay desert earth.
The skulls remain, perhaps some teeth,
the bodies were swallowed,
ingested as quick as one breath,
and above desert grass, some birds,
the wind, the sun, all must keep going,
another day, another day,
no monuments here,
no music played as they were dying,
no hands touching, no burning of incense
or cutting of hair,
no one writing down their last words
or saving their tears in a vial,
no elegy or valediction,
nothing left for a scribe.

Some were thrown in the earth
with their eyes and mouths open,
wrapped in dirty sheets,
no washing of the body,
no song for their journey,
lost between languages,
annihilated, obliterated,
and there would be another day,

13

the town went on the next day.
No Necropolis here,
no yew tree planted
or burials with coins,
no bay leafs on their lips.

Death by drowning,
death by suffocation,
death by being swallowed in the earth.
What does it matter?
Some of their names never recorded,
unknown,
un known,
un to never be to know.
No grave robbers here,
what gold?
what rings?
what medals of honor?
And in the stories, they are forgotten,
barely mentioned, foot notes,
a sentence:
they are the people on one of the seven mesas,
with their short men, dark women, crying babies,
and prayers that sound like curses;
they work to their deaths
because they have families left behind,
because families brought them here,
no interest in making *this place* their home,
visitors only,
grateful for a bed,
grateful for owning chickens,
saying only what is expected
to get that job or that shack of a house.
"You didn't see or hear of the mines or the people in them." *

Burning of the bodies
would include chanting,

a coming together,
a dancing of a tribe,
not a quick way to
remove the dead with no lingering.
Building the pyre would take time,
concentration and planning.
No need for this kind of pause from day-to-day life.
The fire toward heaven,
the release of the body to the infinite,
we will just lift the body and place it in a pine box,
cover it, bury it and then pile more bodies
over that one, cover those,
bury those
and go on,
going about our business in Dawson, New Mexico,
sports games for the children
who do not live on
one of the seven mesas.

* *Coal Town*, Toby Smith, p. 11

Monsters of the Seven Mesas

"Dawson had seven mesas ... and on each of the hills different
nationalities settled, for reasons of social customs and language."
COAL TOWN: THE LIFE AND TIMES OF DAWSON, NEW MEXICO
TOBY SMITH

"All of the Italians they lived up in the canyon ...
I didn't know much about the Italians ."
COAL TOWN: THE LIFE AND TIMES OF DAWSON, NEW MEXICO
TOBY SMITH

A man from the seventh mesa is looking at me,
standing to the north with the sun in his eyes,
on the seventh mesa of the seven mesas they live,
holding a thread as delicate as a strand of hair,
names tangled with other names,
some without names, broken bodies tangled with other bodies,
buried together, weeds choking whatever is left,
and I hear only broken words.

I was not there in Dawson, New Mexico when the mines exploded,
when in 1923 the children in the classroom ask
"What's that?" knowing it was the mine,
a teacher saying it was nothing,
just a thunderstorm or it was just
the sound of a distant train
going to Tucumcari.
But the children know better, and so do the animals.
They smell it before the adults start running to the mine,
before the adults start screaming and crying and cursing
the place (curses still linger in the air here; smell them and pay attention).

Perhaps the same curses
from 1913, the first explosion,
perhaps they pray again to
Our Lady Queen of Angels:
O good and tender Mother,
thou shalt always
be our hope
O Divine Mother,
send thy holy angels
to defend us
and drive far away
*the cruel enemy.**

*"You didn't see or hear of the mines or the people in them." ***

And so it is easy to turn them all into ghosts while they are living,
the white people only had to deal with the disruptions,
a goat running down the main street,
sounds of a language like a fist in the mouth,
the sour smell of chickens in a yard,
someone singing while sweeping the front stoop,
only there to make messes, to be some kind of pain in the ass.

In 1913 it was a way
to become a man,
sons died alone,
sons died with their fathers,
sons who lost fathers that day,
died in 1923 in the other explosion.
Women stood behind a rope,
crying and praying
to the Blessed Virgin Mary:
Queen of angels
Queen of patriarchs
Queen of prophets
Queen of apostles
*Queen of martyrs****

I know this desert does not give
her secrets to just anyone,
and the seven mesas are not giving up
their secrets now,
all the digging must be left
for the poets and the prophets and the sinners:
we who speak for the dead
and sometimes see the dead,
we will bring them back.

* *Prayer to Our Lady Queen of Angels*, dictated to Fr. Cestac, 1864

** *Coal Town*, Toby Smith, p. 11

***The Litany of the Blessed Virgin Mary*, Marian Shrine, Loreto, Italy, 16th century

E Lucevan Le Stelle in Dawson, New Mexico, 1912

" . . . and town officials conscripted a musician named Maldo Coridori from Italy just to conduct a fledgling marching band of coal miners."

COAL TOWN: THE LIFE AND TIMES OF DAWSON, NEW MEXICO

TOBY SMITH

Niccia tries to sing like Enrico Caruso
as she walks out of the darkness into the desert light,
she tells herself it is like opening your eyes
once you reach the surface of the ocean,
after living at the bottom in darkness,
not seeing your own fingers or face
and then suddenly there is this kind of blue
and white shock, and this light;
you can almost feel weighing down on your eyes.
It is almost as painful as being born.

She has never heard Enrico Caruso sing
but her mother heard him in New York
before she took a train and then another and another
until she arrived in Dawson, New Mexico.
Her mother sings *E Lucevan Le Stelle* almost in a whisper:
E lucevan le stelle ed olezzava la terra stridea l'uscio dell'orto . . .
again and again.

Sometimes her mother will start talking about Caruso
and how her *nipote*, her niece, would play the record again and again,
And while her mother sweeps or stirs the bread soup,
she is not really there anymore in that shack,
sweeping dirt from one direction to another,
like a dance,
through the powdery air of coal and dust,

like the perfume of those nights.

"Nicci, do not go near the mine," her mother warns her again and again,
"Women bring *malocchio*, the evil eye, to the mine.
Nobody wants you there."

There is nothing for her to dream about in this place
that always smells like burning coal and *merda*, shit.
"Oh, sweet kisses and languorous caresses…"
she wants to die in desperation for a love she can never have.

Her mother tells her Enrico Caruso was born in Napoli,
a city very close to their *paese*.
If her mother only knew, she would have crawled
on her hands and knees, like a pilgrim to the *Montevirgene*,
just to meet Caruso in Napoli.

But now they are here, no music is heard
except for the Dawson marching band that plays
at baptisms, communions, weddings, and funerals.
While the Italian miners are playing,
her mother closes her eyes and Enrico Caruso is there
the words flying over the body of this strange country,
until they meet with the desert wind of northern New Mexico,
E muoio disperato!
E non ho amato mai tanto la vita,
tanto la vita!
And I die in desperation!
And I never before loved life so much,
loved life so much!

E Lucevan Le Stelle
from the Italian opera, *Tosca*, written by Giacomo Puccini (composer) and
Giuseppe Giacosa & Luigi Illica (lyrics)

St. John the Baptist in Dawson, New Mexico

I am back,
defending the poor, telling the rich
they will never enter heaven,
but I am only speaking to the dead.

Here in this place only
the dead remain to listen
and I do not wait for them to speak.
The graves listen while I speak,
I am the prophet of no one living.
I see the world as good and evil,
I see one way to go, one path,
and no one living wants to
listen to me anymore.
Luddite,
dinosaur,
stick in the mud,
no fun,
somehow I have
lost all relevance.

But the dead—
oh, they understand
what is and what isn't,
what used to be, and what is no longer,
there is no need to explain,
to justify, to defend,
to have to politic for it,
to have to bribe or seduce,
what is greed to the dead?

And yes, it is quiet here,

and sometimes a snake is hiding,
eye catching some of my sounds
and my smells,
but I go on and on,
without taking a breath,
telling my story again and again,
and then all the voices of the dead
start calling out, asking if
I am the one who will take them back,
but their stories are confusing,
no beginning, middle, or end
to any of them.
They don't know when to start
and when to finish,
questions sound like statements,
the grammar no longer exists
and I can't create a map
to follow any of them.
No candles are lit,
and none of them burn mugwort
in prayer, in reverence to me.

So I just go on with my preaching,
my talking and singing,
echoing in circles, waves of sound
penetrating this place like invisible
shock waves passing through,
a mother whale calling out to her baby,
an ocean without water,
only the bones of the dead tremble a bit,
the hissing of silence can barely be heard,
I walk, refusing to leave, looking for what?
I don't know, and how strange because
I used to know. Looking for what?
Who is there to remind me
I am, and have always been,
the warrior of the desert,

and all of you who hear my voice,
you will be saved.

Saturna Finally Speaks

I don't want to remember the smell,
they told me there were worse places
and I needed to be grateful.
How many of us? 9 or 10 . . .I don't remember,
they were careful, calling it a "town"
and not a mining camp.
We were citizens of a town,
and to show our gratitude
we had to be good citizens—no questions, no anger, no protests.
We belonged in a town and like all good American citizens,
we were patriots.

They did not know how to pronounce my name or even spell it,
and now I don't remember.
I would smile and talk in our dialect,
the words are falling between my fingers
like sighs or the wind that I hear
some nights are so dark, so dark
I can only keep my lips moving . . .

But there, in that shack we would talk about our home
that was not this place,
that was across the desert, mountains, an ocean.
I spent so much of my time
sleep-walking, waiting, praying.
I fell asleep on the train when we crossed the border
of Colorado and New Mexico, and did I wake up?

You would say, "Yes, you woke up. Now feed the *piccolina*, and stop with
your *storia dei spiriti*, the dark, the quiet, the moon. *É troppo, é troppo.*
But what I don't tell you in that moment is this:
if I tell myself I am not really here,

that is all I need to know.

O Mother of God, *Mamma Schiavona, Madonna di Montevergine,*
help us find our way back
to where our ancestors are buried.

The grave speaks only to the poet,
but all the poets are gone and there is only me.

When I lived in that shack,
I learned the rules:
do not feed the dead; do not speak in a loud voice;
do not walk outside when you are drunk;
do not let the chickens or the goat in;
do not show anyone the necklace you were given at birth;
do not let anyone speak your name.

They would put me in jail; they would print my name in the newspaper;
they would lie to my children and tell them
I did not know how to clean them;
they (who never spoke my name) gave me all the rules;
I would not question, I would not look them in the eye.

They told us "this is your home" until the day it wasn't anymore.
The rules change; they are not written in blood or bone or stone.
The shack is taken apart plank by plank,
no one cares that I have to leave your grave behind.
That when I try to sleep at night I am choking on the weeds
that are choking your grave.
They never learn my language so they laugh at my stories and my dreams,
and soon they forget my body,
they take apart the church plank by plank
and leave me to the silence of the desert.

I slept for a long time on that train,
but even when I was awake I was dreaming of our home,
you would have stopped trying to teach me English,

you would have stopped moving in lines back and forth.
And now I am dreaming that we are heading east, back to the ocean,
no longer moving in a line from the train to a town
(that is no place really)
to a shack to the mine to the grave to the shack to the train . . .
And we are dancing in circles over the ocean, holding each other up,
all the way back to the piazza and that day we wake up
feeling all life, protection, and joy without question . . .
If I told you then, you would have said *aggio saputo*, I even knew;
I was *una peccata! una pazza!* one who is pitied, a crazy,
and maybe I was.

If I told you how quietly we left Dawson, NM, without you,
so quiet that when I cried, it sounded like whispering or a small cough,
and how they forgot about me,
how they left me out in the cold desert night,
they never even tried to find my body,
they left me to tell my story to no one
and so I speak to no one.

I Forget I Have a Shadow in This Place

Water is my enemy
and this time I cannot turn to my *mama* or *cognate*.
I am on the ship, the *Prinzess Irene*,
three children, Antonio, Assunta, and Filomena,
no bread in this desert ocean,
and as long as sounds came out of my mouth,
I pray on this hot, July day in 1905.

>   *Eight years later in 1913*
>   *a woman falls to the ground*
>   *in Dawson, New Mexico,*
>   *wailing sounds across*
>   *mounds of bodies*
>   *and that woman is me.* *

Everything is swallowed in this place,
even St. John the Baptist
is told to shut his mouth and
va' via, go away.
He cannot conquer,
he cannot speak.

"The first time I step foot on this ground
God should have knocked me down dead . . ."

I tell him again and again,
and he never looks at me,

he goes into that sun
and burns away all our secrets,

I never went to the mine
to that mouth of wanting more and more
until the day it happens,
and there I am in the photograph,
just another "keen wail of a stricken woman
as the body of the pit mouth is identified." **

They never find him,
his body thrown in a mass grave,
I don't know, I was never asked.
Tonight I fry *la torta di polenta*, the cake of bones,
tomorrow we will have *minestra di niente*, soup of nothing.
And I think of my mother telling me
about the bitterness of greens
and what they bring to your life:

rapini
cicoria

She opens my mouth
and shoves those bitter greens in,
"swallow all of it," she says,
"It will make you a bitter woman."

---

* "Remembering the Dawson Mining Disaster, 100 Years Later" Tom Sharpe, The New
Mexican, Oct. 19th, 2013
** *Raton Range*, 1913.

Slow Quiet Stone

for Ottavio Nardini (1882-1913)
and Franco Nardini (1886-1923)

La Facion is still there
eating the evil spirits
that wander through Camporaghena,
the stone village Ottavio and Franco left.

"There is water; I can barely taste it or
maybe it is the stinging nettle,
do not distract me," he commands
as his breath falls over the stones
of every house, the church,
whatever is left.

La Facion does not remember
Ottavio's eyes, but he tells me
"his body has turned to stone,"
and then mentions, "the priest
who tried to hide in a chestnut tree,
the tree is there for protection,
the tree is there to carry you
through your life, but they found him that day.
I could not stop all of them that day."

There is silence after that confession, and
I remind *La Facion* the priest was executed years
after Ottavio was killed in New Mexico.

"The chestnuts are very important," he announces,
"they must be protected always, the roots of the trees
might remember Ottavio."

Did the trees talk to Ottavio?
All of that is lost along with the protection he had,
when he made the journey over the ocean
and arrived in Dawson, New Mexico.
All he had were the dreams of how
the water tasted in Camporaghena, Italy.

"He is stone now," La Facion states as a fact,
and he knows about stones.
He uses the stones in this village to protect.
"That is my job," he says,
he is guarding what I cannot see
and there is a lot I cannot see.

"Don't ask me what happened to them
in the desert," *La Facion* says
as his breath moves over my face,
I am too close to him now,
he knows how to scare anyone living
or whatever is dead.
"Spirits move on but sometimes
they grow roots, make a claim.
Don't ask me."

Before Ottavio and his younger brother,
Franco, left the village for America,
two spirits jump in, demanding
a ride across the ocean.
But the old woman took care of it,
a chestnut for each brother,
two small hearts in the hand,
"questo è per te
e questo è per te,"
this is for you
and this is for you.

* *La facion: a stone face attached to doors and windows for protection against evil spirits.*

** *"Prominent in Camporaghena village is the Church of St. Peter and St. Paul from the 12th century. On the church piazza there's a very moving tribute to a parish priest, Don Lino Baldini, who was executed by the Nazis. On July 4, 1944, the priest rang the church bells to warn the population of an impending Nazi reprisal, an action for which he was murdered, along with four other civilians."*

I Had Left Even Their Spirits Behind Me

"The wagon jolted on, carrying me I know not whither . . .
If we never arrived anywhere it did not matter."
WILLA CATHER, *MY ANTONIA*

for Anne Hutchinson (1591-1643)

My fingers have been bleeding all day,
I stand by the tree in front of my house
and wait for the news.
I will not talk in their language anymore:
       walking in tiny steps to the wagon
       walking over the frozen land,
       the mouth of the Lord hath spoken it.

Three hundred years later,
you will get a tongue,
hands will push you out
in a hospital,
in New Rochelle, New York,
so close to
where I will be killed.

You start your breathing in the same air,
you smell the Long Island Sound,
it is an animal always there on your skin.
You hear the waves at night
and you want to tell me "Listen!"
but it is too late for me, little girl,
the wagon is taking me into the forest,
the land here does not speak back to me,
God's hand presses heavy
on my shoulder, and I will

continue my work.

While you dance
the *tarantella*
night after night,
you invite me in,
hold out your arms,
call to me, sing to me,
gather all the children

But my child was only
a knot of blood and flesh,
for others to examine,
never given a chance,
never could hold that small body,
a small body that became
their sigil of evil.

But I am talking of the Lord
and I continue my need to define
what is legal grace in this land
and what is evil,
and I tell them:
"If you go on in this course you begin,
you will bring a curse upon you and your posterity . . ."
you, you all, "the mouth of the Lord hath spoken it."

One of my daughters,
will not be killed that day;
she will hide at Split Rock,
she will leave
even the spirits
behind her;
she will learn
a new language;
she will not remember
what it means

to be homesick,
she will look at the land
and decide not to pray.

Nino's Mother

"...The *Elizabeth* struck
one of these bars, off Fire Island beach, at around 3:30 a.m.
on July 19, 1850."

PAULA BLANCHARD, *MARGARET FULLER:*
FROM TRANSCENDENTALISM TO REVOLUTION

My name is Margaret.
Tired, I dip bread in the soup,
lick the spoon, lick my fingers.

I smell his skin, his wide face in the dark,
mouth open here he is waiting for our trip,
I move into the shadows before he starts
to shake his head out of a dream.

My son cries today,
"Voglio Mamma, voglio Mamma, dov'è?"
the water cradles his body now,
but his skin is not used
to this kind of touch.

It wants to swallow him, a growing monster,
invites him into her belly.
I have to let him go finally
while the land forms an edge to our love.

He begs for *un biscotto e un bacio,*
the wind is in his mouth and
we hear the wood groaning.

"Ti voglio bene," he hears over and over,
first a shout and then it stretches to a cry, a whisper,

I tell him to put his chin down
and his eyes close

for naps in our dark warm room,
his thumb in his mouth
and he would ask for a mother.

I see him blurring under my fingers,
biting on the shutter,
as the sun dips down away from his window,
he smelled of me that day.

La Befana

So cold.
I walk with the dead,
I am not their leader or their god,
I am not on the hunt.
They have heard enough about
where they are going,
where they have been,
and why should they care anymore?
All lies. I know that
as I was not in a straight line,
not in the solid dark of this night,
here we are in that in-between time,
but you don't know yet what
I am talking about. That is okay.

I was fierce.
Do any of you remember?
No one here to talk to,
language is no longer the currency,
so you need to save the talk
for some other time,
for what might be ahead for you
and for us.

Each step in this desert
means we are between
light and dark,
did I hear the ocean?
I taste the sea water in my mouth
but that is only because I am here,
and because we are going down.

They used to call us "The Army of Diana"
but no one knows her;
we were told a man leads
the soldiers of the dead,
but there are no soldiers here.
And if the children could speak,
they would cry
so I am grateful for their loss.

I will not tell you where I have been
as I rise from my bed this dawn,
it is a secret I keep
on the tip of my tongue,
a tiny bone that no one can see
unless I finally open my mouth.

PART TWO

atterrá . . .

"Memory (the deliberate act of remembering) is
a form of willed creation. It is not an effort to find
out the way it really was—that is research. The
point is to dwell on the way it appeared and why it
appeared in that particular way."

TONI MORRISON, "MEMORY, CREATION, AND FICTION"

Wall Cloud (Driving from
New Mexico to South Dakota)

"Have you ever seen a wall cloud?"
such a look of disinterest, boredom in the room
and I know I left a piece of myself somewhere on that highway
after we drove out of Rosebud.
Running away and in that act pushing myself
and my daughter to the very edge.
No one understands here.

I am the stranger here. Before we left Rosebud I was not.
The houses, the children running,
it could have been Santo Doming or Cochiti. I was alright.
I am in a car with my friend and daughter.
The space is inviting to me. It is the northern sky;
we will see the Northern lights in the winter.
I think of Canada and movement,
none of this stuck in one place, fires surrounding us
as if we were in hell already
and the poverty is the same really.
Isn't that what we all think?

And then it is there, building on the horizon.
The young man at the gas station mentioned a tornado warning up north.
I thought he was trying to scare us:
two white women who don't even have a cell phone.
(I want to tell him, "I am not that kind of white woman"
the kind wandering around a reservation
who believes she is protected by privilege, a kind of leather on skin.)
I did not believe him. That was my first mistake.

We appear to be driving right into it.
I start to think it looks like judgment.
It looks like what we have always following behind us,
floating only inches to the left or right,
touching our shoulder as we sleep in our beds.
As we stare out a window and think of wet graves,
it is there breathing and waiting.
It looks like the empty room that echoes once all of your furniture
is gone and there is some hair floating in the dust.
Where are you? Does anyone remember?
No ceremony? Can no more be done?
It is now only land and sky, brutal on the heart,
you are nothing here.
"What is that?" I ask,
remembering rain falling in straight lines over a distant mesa.

It is a wall cloud,
and some poverty tastes different on your tongue,
and I have lost the markers along the road,
and now we are near a ditch,
and the car is shaking,
and I have run into a wall
when I only thought I was trading in
summers of fire
and unburied skeletons of women,
for some kind of healing.

La Vergine (Madison, South Dakota)

It is December 12th, the feast day of *La Vergine*,
the Serpent Goddess who battles for us,
the Lady of Heaven who weeps for us,
the Black Madonna who bleeds for us;
here in Madison, South Dakota, where houses stand
silent as stares without a tasting of blood,
the wind from the north is all we hear for comfort
and the stars unblinking and so far away from anything human.
Some wintered people rumbling into cars this icy early morning,
shaped by the landscape where there is no need to make a spectacle.
My daughter wrapped in her coat and scarf, asks me
why do people crawl up the steps to the church on this day,
and it breaks my heart knowing the genetic landscape she shares
with her ancestors, who also walked barefoot for *La Vergine*,
who kneeled and prayed for hours:
my mother, grandmothers, great-grandmothers.
My fingers hold the frozen steering wheel,
my daughter's dark eye holding a frozen curse,
lacking the words, the knowing of what to do.

I can only speak of sacrifice, humility,
abstracted language I have used in a classroom;
telling a ten-year-old shivering girl the need for ritual:
some kind of gesture marking our own insignificance in this world,
expressing with our bodies the devotion to something larger.
My words are swallowed in the cold dark morning air
as we drive into the empty street, passing unadorned churches;
in this landscape of white on white, we are the closeted volcano,
how vulgar to cry for a statue, how unnecessary to crawl.

This Desert

On February 2, 2009, a woman walking a dog found a human bone on
the West Mesa of Albuquerque, New Mexico metropolitan area, and
reported it to police. As a result of the subsequent police investigation,
authorities discovered the remains of 11 women and an unborn fetus
buried in the area. All the women were young; most were Hispanic, and
most were involved with drugs and prostitution.

WIKIPEDIA

This has been the summer of bones,
it doesn't matter which direction the wind comes from,
we are covered in the dust,
we could be walking around a half-constructed housing development,
and find the buried women, a baby, all silent and waiting for us,
they are speaking with the spirits of Pompeii or Chaco Canyon,
the dead will try to talk to us, but at some point
they realize that we are too busy for that kind of conversation
so they patiently wait for us to notice.
It takes time, years before the layers are removed
to enter the heart of all this
on the west side of Albuquerque, a place that
creates dreams of having the loving wife and husband,
two children, and a pool in the desert,
less than two miles from volcanoes that are
also silently waiting for us to notice.

After the girls are murdered and buried,
all that time I walk from my house to my car,
glancing up at the sky, worried I am going to be late,
and they are waiting;
all that time I talk on the phone and glance toward the west,
toward the setting sun,
not seeing any horses of eternity or hearing the terrible voice of God,

they are waiting as I drive west on the interstate
caught in my own tangle of stories of
what happened and who said what and why,
they are waiting,
and words are of no use anymore,
language becomes what is left of the bodies.
We can only find meaning sifting through the bones,
piece by piece.

These daughters slipped away, one by one,
disappearing in some file, and we continued driving our cars
and shopping, our lives did not skip a heart beat with each disappearance.
Now we still do not remember their names and look at the faces
as we go on with our routines and comment on
how sad it all is or how tragic.
The parents appear on camera, looking uncomfortable and lost,
their faces asking for acceptance and forgiveness,
and yet we do not see us in them; we can say our daughters
will not end up murdered and dumped at the bottom of a mesa,
we know we are not like them,
we create the gated community,
the walls of privilege so our daughters will not be
taken away by a monster, they will know better,
we will protect them with our money and the idea
that we are better..

The daughters are here, uncovered, ready to tell us what they know,
they are hoping that others may speak for them,
they are asking for Mother-Isis or Kali-Ma to speak
the words we can understand in the middle of a dream or prayer:

This desert is not always a mother's breast
or even the comfort of her arms,
it has teeth and will eat our young,
it is something beautiful and terrible,
when we must all dance our way back
to the black heart of the mother.

Walking to El Santuario de Chimayó, New Mexico

We have walked for days but my mother does not look tired,
I begin to notice the crosses but cannot find the words
to explain what each cross means and how it arrived in this place.
My mother is blinking and then I realize that we will never get there,
not as we wind along the snakelike path.
The stars that were looking without emotion or metaphor,
fade into the desert morning sky. We have already lost our way,
but no one is talking.
And then I remember that we have already lost our language
somewhere between the coast of Campania and this prehistoric ocean.

But we are not the first. It begins with a dream at Chaco Canyon
when too many people are trying to talk to me,
and then listening to one person talk about my dead father
and pointing to a mountain.
Every invasion perhaps starts with a dream,
the warning of who will arrive and who must be massacred.
The massacre comes in all kinds of disguises and trickery.
"We can't live here anymore."
"Another *terramoda*."
"They won't let us live here anymore."
"Another *guerra*."
Another slippery promise that is created with language
but has no use for metaphor or dream.

Some of us are forced to re-interpret when there is no way,
walking on that road with my mother, we do not find a goddess,
only tumbleweed and trash thrown from cars.
"Is this the way?" I ask but she does not answer.
"*Ma dov'è andiamo?*" But where are we going?
and that is the question of the century.

"*È niente.*" It is nothing, but is that true?
Is it all nothing as we go on talking into the darkness,
entering the cave and knowing we will never see sky again.

On this pilgrimage we walk in circles, knowing
there is no beginning point and no final point on the map.
Every canyon we climb down and every mesa in the distance
is metaphor for whatever. I can create the meaning
since I am the re-translator in this story.

It has been a long trip but I stopped counting the days
and only remember the images.
The rush of the ocean water crushing down on the parking lot
announcing "I am here" to all the startled people in their cars.
That was another dream but it might not mean anything,
that was what I thought about in the middle of suburbia
or the image of all of us drowning on the Long Island Expressway.
Again no one expecting it and a look of "How could you?" as if
we are somehow protected because of what we buy and where we live.
But here in this desert all the voices arrive, some wait for night
and others are here walking with us,
un viaggio dei morti, a journey of the dead
and I remember the tiny bird who is landing
outside of my window, fragile wing and head,
coming out of nowhere
like a tiny bug who arrives to give us a message,
startling us after a bath or standing in the middle of the kitchen,
this bird is chirping, smaller than a child's hand,
announcing the news
but we have already left
following the others into the desert.

Making Light, Crownpoint, New Mexico

My son asks me as we turn off the exit to Thoreau,
"Where are we now, Mama?"
I can see Mt. Taylor in my rearview mirror at least in this dream,
and I can only say we are here now.
I have cried on this road already,
the Continental Divide cracking through my body,
never understanding the presence of wind until now,
walking awake or sleeping
it doesn't matter,
the wind rises up in the night, a larger body than the sky,
refusing me to find an edge
over and over again until early daylight.

This dry afternoon the wind attacks
taking whatever water is left;
I have been invaded,
dried soul, no whisper of what was underneath all this dirt,
I submerge in an ocean, salty, heavy,
water covering my face, my breasts,
what kind of place is this?
the harshest place in the world,
taking you to the point when you can see
you no longer exist,
where there is nowhere to run anymore,
where you never existed.

I find someone who can talk about fingers,
feeling the face like it is a piece of pottery,
he will also lose what is left of him in a few years
after I am gone.
but we don't know that this afternoon,
I tell him the wind is closing in on me,

the wind has become my enemy,
I tell him too many people have walked this place,
too many prayers and whispers,
and I tell him I won't be able to sleep again at night.
He only smiles and says, "I see."

I find myself rolling from one ancient landscape to another,
Italy to Crownpoint is a long way,
the soil has turned to rock,
the heart has fossilized,
bones are scattered and no longer mark a birthplace,
a finger pushed me across the ocean, across the country,
and I cannot find a center, a matrix to this language.
My son can find a macrofossil against that hill,
we could create another macrocosm,
rubbing our hands across a whale jawbone,
waiting for the comet that marks the end of a century
like an eye on a map.

One Sunday night driving from Albuquerque to Crownpoint,
my son sleeps and my breathing, his breathing anchors us,
the stars higher than the black mesa, silent, the black mesa
catches our small sounds and only echoes back its sound, no language,
passing people continuously feeding the graves in Thoreau,
I push my son up to the surface of the ocean,
helping him to breathe here,
"Mama, I don't like Crownpoint," but I push him,
we move together, making our ancient path as we have done before,
swimming above the bones of our family.

Memento (Crownpoint, New Mexico)

The snow falls like whispers
on your black hair,
you stay warm traveling
from your building to Farmington,
your mother sick,
but you say very little to me.

I only imagine
what kind of son you are,
after you left home
for a few years,
you told me you needed to return.

Here we meet
in front of the mesa,
children who translate
need from *want*,
in our dying languages,
we starve for music,
good food,
and for that place
we desire always:
cradlesong.

I stay in bed this weekend,
I do not want to hear
the wind anymore,
its lungs lumbering above me,
howling for hours,
I shrink into a knot,
knuckle under to survive.

I have to drive
an hour to Grants
for my son who will
later on cry
and vomit in the car.

You drive away in your truck,
following the campus road
out to the highway
until you reach
your mother.

I wonder if that ever happened
to you: the belonging,
I mean.

After my mother died
I cried for the death,
and years later I realized
my baby language
was buried with her.

Every morning is a kind of fog
until I walk across the icy parking lot
to the library
to you behind the counter,
a librarian in the desert
looking fresh and alive,
after a two-hour car drive.

We talk about gourmet coffee
and I curse the on-again, off-again wifi.

Your mother was still alive at that time.

I plant a garden in the clay soil,
digging and hauling in dirt,

plants that should have grown tall
are stunted, bent to a side.

Spanish broom in a pot, that was a mistake,
roses in this place, what was I thinking.

It takes me hours to dig a hole,
but I am not listening, not yet.

It all died when I left.

When I walk to your apartment for some answers,
we have become the stunted people,
we hunger to stay upright for maybe a day.
You tell me what you want in a wife,
and I say *thank you* and leave.

Perhaps you have a wife, a child,
perhaps you sip on peyote and carry a bible,
and maybe you finally cut your hair.

I lay in the dark, a cold finger on my aching right hip,
our circle of breath appearing and disappearing
in that canyon, without us knowing, without anyone
telling our story, without any memory in the rock.

Continental Divide(s)

I talk about my mother, and her mother,
and so many mothers before that,
barely swimming across borders,
drowning after their feet touched ground,
"My mother, she no like this *countree*,"
and I cry along with Cather's Antonia,
her frozen father left behind with the animals,
the men who must hack away at his frozen blood.

"My mother, she no want this *countree*,"
and there is my mother talking to her mother
in a whisper, "this country is *merda*,"
"this country is shit,"
and yet here we are,
turning into motherless drifters,
creating nothing out of dollar bills,
and no one stops running.
They never tell you that before you leave.

When I cross the Continental Divide, the air shifts
and my body must adjust to sudden gusts of wind,
I am no longer in one country or another,
for a moment I lose control and then it is over,
an old man stands by the highway divider,
waving his hand at me,
and I wave back without thinking.

We have to learn to talk to ghosts
when we cross from one continent to another.
I did not learn that from my mother or her mother,
they found a spot
and stayed there, unwilling to move.

They had done enough traveling
for so many lifetimes, leaving behind
bodies, voices, and smells of that place,
that place that told them who they were;
now they say every car trip is just too long.

Driving away from the Valley of the Fires,
we ask only for forgiveness out here,
buried scars in the old Oscura Mountains,
I am surprised to see cows bending their heads,
cacti flowers trembling in the wind,
none of that should be here at ground zero,
not after what we have done.

I give you this invitation to follow us,
down another road, moving beyond the
borders of your own skin,
do not look to us for answers,
we only hold a stick
to poke at what
might destroy us all.

Confession

"Grief is a land of wet tenderness."

JOY HARJO

Driving on Interstate 25, the light barely stretches across
to the Sandia Mountains, whispering the evening
to the white cross that marks where one of my students died,
another I saw tonight, another daughter,
I told her father she is a good human being.
I watched her give my daughter a blue teddy bear
and my daughter dropping it again and again, waiting for her
to pick it up again.
All of us breathing under the fluorescent light,
reaching with some hope on our faces.
In the car I feel God pressing her heavy heart down on my face,
this is the only way,
feeding your child,
washing her feet in the bathroom sink,
helping a student understand
there is no such thing as a wrong poem.
We are always confessing our lives to each other
without words, through our bodies, our fingers that reach or push away,
our hands that release or hold,
in what we almost do with our eyes,
and what we are afraid to reveal in the early morning light,
our bodies almost breathing in fresh life
while the dreams sink heavy below us
as we rise and slowly meet what story we are creating.

I have spent the night confessing to the spirits,
who were not sleeping,
who woke me at midnight to remind me of all this.
I carry the pain and remember my mother's lips,

I wet her mouth with ice in that hospital room
which did not allow her history to sink in,
her garden waiting at home for digging or revelation,
the placenta slow dancing from my mother to me to my daughter;
I told my mother that Grandma showed up in my dream,
seaweed curled around her fingers, she spoke to me in Italian,
telling me my mother would be alright;
under a full moon my daughter will hide in a bathroom,
wondering who to call for an offering or the light touch of a finger.

The day my student was buried,
the parking lot around the church was full,
the main street lined with cars,
I pushed my daughter in her stroller,
flies hitting my face in the hot noon heat,
we walked past a Family Dollar store,
I found her drinking cup, I wiped her face,
I was holding on to her as if we were eternal points on a map
never moving regardless of earthquake or drought.

Tonight the shadows grow around us,
as car lights float away, the volcanoes disappear,
the river falls away in a night prayer,
my daughter and I drive in darkness, no edges,
no map, no way for us to see.

Hekate's Hitch

"With her came one who takes various shapes, having three heads,
a deadly monster you do not wish to know: Hecate of Tartartus."

THE ORPHIC ARGONAUTICA, JASON COLARITO (TRANS.)

Each direction has its danger
at the crossroads here in forgotten town,
border-town Gallup, New Mexico.

We might meet her at the crossroads,
downtown where the trains keep coming and going,
in the alley behind the American Bar.
She would be gathering the lost and the taken,
the living and the dead,
the ones who stopped talking,
and the ones who walk in all directions.
She will be walking the tracks.

Italian hands laid down
the cathedral stones in this town,
they did not know about the crossroads here,
but they knew about evil, and about blood,
and they fed what they could to the spirits they saw.
Throughout the day they sang and told jokes
to keep *il malocchio* away.
They were here and then gone,
but their voices join the parade here night after night,
the vanished,
the unsettled,
the ones without tongues,
the ones between life and death.

As we call on Hekate with our garlic and our prayer,

let us all be careful,
there is no water here only dust,
she is not quite a woman, not quite.
And she is not the Mary who weeps.
No, Hekate leaves her throne empty for others to find,
and the snake that protects her garden
follows her to this desert of *animas*,
the spirits linger and wait.

We hear her wail
and here is our warning:
we should not look at her
because anything might happen
like the destruction of the world.
One breath from her mouth
and all breaths will follow:
Leave your throne and find us,
root out the danger
with your fennel stalk,
and walk the tracks with us.

Blood Moon

Athena, Wall-e, and I
under a blood moon in eclipse
in Gallup, New Mexico;
we are silent because
we do not speak each other's languages.
Athena smells like cat piss,
Wall-e howls in his sleep,
and I have fingers and
the tongue to tell stories:
so here is another one of my stories.

Athena has her back to the moon,
climbing up a tree,
who cares?
She is playing and it is 6
in the morning in this border-town,
unlike Wall-e and me,
Athena was born here
behind a shed,
her white fur running
like a baby spirit
all around the driveway and street,
despite the hanging moon looking like
another planet,
it is nothing to her.

She was almost trapped on a roof
when she was a baby, but she flew down
and landed near her mother and brother.

Wall-e is attached to a leash,
he has no place to go

except where I pull him;
he is low to the ground,
smelling some old shit from another dog,
the blood moon gives him no story, no way out.
But Wall-e, born in South Dakota,
knows all the smells of snow,
knows how snow mats on his fur,
knows the taste of that metal cold,
it takes him back.

I am already creating a story here,
the blood moon looks like the
inside of my mother's mouth
or the sound of language
when I cried in my crib.
I was born near the ocean
and now in this desert town,
the moon is a menacing ocean to me,
blood washing over the three of us,
I did not expect to be baptized
this early in the day,
but when I saw it and said "Oh."

PART THREE

rispetto . . .

"... *rispetto* was a humbling and humble
acknowledgment of things as they are, a recognition
of what is. Work, time, and other people were to be
respected because they were all inescapably real.
The idea also carried connotations of reciprocity,
an insistence on shared responsibility and mutually
recognized dignity."

ROBERT ANTHONY ORSI, *THE MADONNA OF 115TH STREET*

Cry Baby

I ask my teacher a question,
"Stop whining. Go sit down."
My face is hot. I want to cry but don't.
I sit on the stool and sink into
another version of myself.
"Crybaby," my mother calls me,
saying in Italian worse, "*Piscia occhio*,"
peeing from your eye;
she would laugh at me and still I would cry,
her small feet pointing out like two swollen little soldiers,
my river surrounding her but never drowning her.

In high school my Social Studies teacher cries in class
about what the war has done,
we are there in the story
when his friend's head explodes.
I try not to move in my seat and I feel like I can't breathe,
no one calls him a fairy for crying, crying like a little girl.
My math teacher stands by the door with a yardstick
and hits every student who does not have the homework.
I will not cry in front of her as I walk past her angry face,
my mouth stays closed all day at school,
afraid to open it even to eat, even to speak.

In college my professor tells me
my paper on Wordsworth's poem
is misguided,
mistaken,
miserable.
Do I even know what I am talking about?
He does not cry when he tells me all of this,
but he looks like he wants to.

I sit and listen, pretend I understand
all the scrawling red words,
as if I really do have a place in this world
of romanticism,
modernism,
and post-modernism;
it is not a place for tears,
I am an English major and
I cannot cry in that classroom.

At my grandmother's funeral mass,
all my uncles are crying,
standing in the front of the altar by the coffin,
while the priest prays in Italian,
our mother tongue, and now we are burying
the mother of all of us.
Uncle Mike, Uncle Tony, Uncle George,
Uncle Dave, and Uncle John
are all sobbing, no swallowing,
no choking back:
they are the babies and so are we all,
crying for *la mamma*,
no one announces, "Enough of that."

I read a poem in a graduate class
about my mother,
before she dies,
before I spent a week in the ICU
watching her die.
When I am done reading,
a woman is crying,
she never cries when she reads her own poems,
there might be a pause before she states,
"And then he slaps me."

I don't understand her poems
but I pretend to understand,

I need to belong in this
white, neutral space.

Everyone knows I am pretending,
everyone knows I am still that dark girl
falling in that closet
in the porch that wasn't a porch,
where I hurt myself,
and I am crying,
and my mother is yelling,
"*Ma, che so c'è se?*"
"What the heck happened?"
and it starts again.

Going to the Farm

"Who are you indeed who would talk or sing to America?"

WALT WHITMAN, *BY BLUE ONTARIO'S SHORE*

Can a little girl sing to her America
while sitting in the back seat of a
Chevrolet station wagon
and all they are doing is driving
east on Long Island to the farm?
That is the place where her parents buy bushels of tomatoes,
to make the sauce they will eat the rest of the year,
and one or two bushels of peaches,
and while they are driving back home,
her mother passing her a peach,
one after another,
her poison,
her death,
and when she is eating her third one,
she breaks out in hives,
and her eyes burn and itch.
the half-eaten peach drops heavy in her lap,
crying with the peach juice
around her mouth,
her father does not look back and keeps driving,
her mother turns around,
"*Ma, che so c'è se?*"
meaning "But, what is happening?"
meaning "What did you do now?"
she can't talk because of the sobs
and all the peach in her mouth,
as they drive by potato farms, roots dried out in piles
across the fields and open space
that soon will be only ghosts,

is this where she sings?

Sometimes her Uncle Mike would take a ride
with her grandmother and they all went to the farm;
it felt like a holiday when it was just a Sunday.
Driving almost two hours from Harrison, New York
in Westchester County to Deer Park New York
in Suffolk County on Long Island
for tomatoes, peaches, corn.
It felt like a celebration like when her parents
would drive a few hours to upstate New York
for cherries. Then they would stop at a rest area
and eat cherries, her mother saving some of the pits
to plant in the yard.

Now the developments are there,
Meadow Acres, Paradise Hills, Valley of the Shadow,
more and more of whatever,
and her parents are now buried in the cemetery,
a quick turn off the exit they passed by
every time they drove out to the farm.

She no longer can live there,
choosing to make her claim
under the drought of dried bones of an old desert and an ancient ocean,
here in Albuquerque, she takes her two children
to Wagoner's Farm in Corrales, New Mexico every October,
the time of the dead,
caring for the skulls, all that is left,
but her children run around looking for pumpkins
and they can smell the green chili roasting,
she smells a tomato but she buys a red chili ristra for the porch,
only ghosts now in her head,
she can hear their voices,
her Uncle Mike calling her by her nickname, "Millie Boss"
he had the same twitching eye that her grandmother had,
no one in this place knows them,

no one can hear the broken *Napolitana* they spoke,
but as she gets older
she feels their breath on her neck,
while she looks at the distant volcanoes
that are just waiting for their next time.

Remembering You in Truth or Consequences, New Mexico

That Saturday morning I woke up in your small bed,
realizing you had sat at your desk all night studying.
We had been two legs of a compass
and now you were no longer speaking my language:

"I brought a heart into the room,
   But from the room, I carried none with me;"

Waking in the morning, entangled in each other again and again,
two scared kids from Long Island,
what did I know:

"Who will believe me, if I swear . . . That I would have had the plague a year?"

For years, I would not know,
I did not realize my time was up.

Even the Christmas when you gave me
a skirt set, golden beige,
holding it against me,
an older woman—career girl—
already my time was up,
swallowing me up
the message in that gift box,
the gift a saleswoman helped you find:
"you mean nothing, I will leave you
in a month or a year—it is coming."

I was swallowed whole that morning
in your frat room in that building
on Massachusetts Avenue, Cambridge, Massachusetts.

I looked down into the alley—
dark brick and the smell of urine,
and up to the gray sky—
stretching my small body in your bed,
I felt warm before the kill:

"He swallows us, and never chews:
  By him, as by chain-shot, whole ranks do die,"

I had brought you every war story,
stitch by stitch, bone by bone
and none of it mattered,
that old lady me should have warned me
when she read my Tarot cards,
I was wasting my time.

"broken glasses show a hundred lesser faces"

and this morning alone in my bed
with only a sheet covering me like a shroud
It is only in this heating up, silent room, I understand.

I open the door to the desert sun,
blasting heat and light
forcing its way
into my face and body,
I enter.

* Lines from John Donne's sonnet, "The Broken Heart"

My Father is Laughing

We are drowning from a week of rain,
a lake surrounds the house
as I drive your car to the supermarket.
We need bread and club soda for dinner.
I see your eyeglasses under the car radio,
I smell the old car grease on a rag near my feet,
and I realize this is all I can take with me
back to the desert.

You were angry when you had the stroke,
yelling at the television at some woman,
at least that is what my mother said.
Now that you are dead, I can call you a miser
and say whatever the hell I want in this poem.

I do remember the day you held me in the Long Island Sound,
you were not a good swimmer,
but you told me to hold on to your neck
as we went in so deep into this animal of water and breath.
I did not slip for a moment,
looking back at the island,
looking up at the sky
that day.

You were a words-in-the-face kind of man,
handing me a lecture on long phone calls,
wasting electricity,
you were always wrestling every bill
under that yellow kitchen light,
sometimes a moth around your head,
yelling about no money in the bank,
and did we think you were made of money?

I was told that in the I.C.U. you accepted Christ,
admitting to all that God was stronger,
but were you laughing then or after?
There could not have been words,
only eyes moving,
and that sweaty minister was there
along with my born-again half-brother
who was determined that you were going
to meet Jesus in heaven,
you were broken
and all rejoiced.

I have nothing to say about this new father
except that you left me when I was 35 years old,
and now I have photographs
but they are not you yelling about taxes
and hypocrites,
laughing at those church weddings and all
the phony Christians,
I wish your photographs would annoy me,
but they are only shadows of what you were.

Walking to the mouth of your grave,
sinking in the mud and grass,
what is left from the flood,
brings me to this:
I was given a gift from you:
the smile that says we are all ridiculous,
scratching your head while saying "no" and "yes."

The Mother and The Seeds

The sand in the south valley of Albuquerque
does not need my help this spring,
a windy dry Palm Sunday weekend,
a year after my father died.
I have resisted gardening for a long time,
I would rather feel the sand in my mouth,
the air stinging my eyes on the edge of a mesa and a landfill.
No one really knows what is buried out there in the west,
it will take years before they start discovering
the young women's bodies.

My mother holds a bag of seeds in the garage,
she tells me she doesn't know what to do with them.
"The grass has taken over the garden," she says,
(as it should take over the world)
"I can't bend over anymore, I fall down."

We walk in the snow on this island where I was born,
my mother has no boots and steps in my footsteps,
the snow is up to our knees.
I have the number of the row and headstone,
my mother stops, she can't breathe,
she jokes that this would be the best place to die,
we would save some money, we could just throw her in a hole.
I keep going until I am standing over my father's half-year grave,
the wind wants to lift me over the headstone, but I stand,
a small marker of gravity, nothing more really,
just like how he is nothing more,
no more voice, no more waving a hand, "forget about it,"

no more hands lined with black car grease years after
he had stopped working.
And we are left with nothing more than these small objects
no one will buy: a worn out wallet, rusty tools, old eyeglasses,
bundles of seeds tied up in rags, jars with rusted caps,
there is no library of books, no art work worth millions,
it is all in a falling down garage with an old stove
and piles of shopping bags and newspapers.
I bury the seashells and let the wind lift me up;
my mother goes back to the car and says
she thought she was going to fall down.
And in a few years she will fall down
and that will be that, as well.

I take my son to the ocean and we gather winter sand
for a man who wrote me a love poem and
talked to me about how he wants to die
under layers of quilts with family around,
but he is gone after I make my first mistake,
sifting through my fingers, I do not even
remember his words anymore.
Now I hold nothing but air as I listen to the wind
pushing off the mesa blowing the sand back and forth
against the windows like a beast breathing,
like the ocean wave that always remains,
taking us back one breath at a time.

Una Storia

My great-grandfather sat at the table
eating cheese,
calling every priest who came near him
a "*mangiapane.*"

When he died, they lifted his body
off the bed
and placed him on the floor,
to flatten the sheets,
to sharpen the razored corners,
and then they put him back.

He was sitting up
sipping wine
before he died.
My mother stood in the doorway
and watched.

She tells me
while we sit in the living room
watching a soap opera
as I squirm in my school clothes:
that he was a good man,
that he cracked nuts with his teeth.

Grandma Rinaldi

You walk by the highway
on the way to Albuquerque,
your feet move in a seaward dance
you brought from *San Giorgio del Sannio*
to this desert.
Voices on the ship
sing amputation,
the steps to the cemetery,
the electric candles you will never see.
This is another place:
the rocks here can be piled for a grave,
and the cross on the mountain
is the bedspread you made,
once I was married
and finally had a bed.

Your large hand cracks the sky
when you wave at me in the car,
at my birth,
your wedding day,
the night you whispered your son's coffin,
the afternoon of my death,
and I write the message for my mother,
who is now sleeping in Deer Park, Long Island,
moving her lips to the whales,
turning the ship into a baby.

When I visited your house
before last winter or after,
we never talked.
I could have told you
your food cut down into my stomach,

pulling out every cell of who I though I was.
I could have told you about my lady in the backyard,
the muffled mouth of the wind through my bedroom wall,
even then the mountains, the city were waiting.
You asked me, "*Ma, che vuoi?*"
"come on, what do you want?"
your twitching eye accusing my mother
of never satisfying my hunger.

We dance together from grave to bed
holding the bones of another memory:
you will make a soup
forcing life into a body
and I will make a cup
for someone to hold at this time.

The Last Rinaldi Brother

for Tony Rinaldi (1930-2017)

died this February,
the last breath,
did you hear it?

Above all the noise of the day,
did you hear?
going and gone,
no shock to my system
in the middle of my day,
a message on my cell phone
and I go on walking to my office,
answering questions,
never stopping
until I write this,
"I lost almost all my world today."

The language I opened my eyes to,
the first food in my mouth,
disappeared today,
did I hear it?

Forrester Street, Albuquerque, NM: A Sestina

"And so we move as far
As Enemies—away—
Just looking round to see how far
It is—Occasionally—"

EMILY DICKINSON

We wander through the dark
the light of jack-o-lanterns help us find the ground
my son and daughter are floating away without a sign.
Which disguises are we wearing this year?
I only think of my aching feet in that moment,
never realizing this is ending now, the last time.

How would I have known it would be the last time,
not taking seriously what was coming for us in the dark.
Avoiding the uneven sidewalk that last year in a moment

my daughter tripped over, and screaming, she hit the ground,
I tried to comfort her, but she would not stop crying that year,
and now we are back, and negligent mother, I do not notice the signs.

As we maneuver around crowds, no one holds up a sign,
"Wake up, this is it, you have run out of time."
I only long for my couch because there will always be another year,
I want to be laid down, and put to rest through this heavy autumnal dark,
but wait, someone should have shaken me, pushed me to the ground,
"Wake up, remember the smells, the candles lit in this moment."

We walk past the doll and her bloody mouth, glass eyes that pin the moment,
a dust bowl high chair and a requiem that swells up to a wall cloud sign
for us to hear, the owner's masterpiece, he creates this holy ground,
no candy, no one asks in this place and time,
it is not a place for fun, tricking or treating banishes-- it is a pilgrimage in the dark,
and it is the place we find ourselves year after year.

Like gravestones that mark that certain day and year,
but soon become hiding places for children, they lose their significant moment,
we walk down Forrester Street believing we are ahead of the dark,

holding out our bags of candy, laughing along with every sign.
My daughter is a princess, my son a Ninja, and we ignore the time,
when their hands will escape me, and I will spiral down to the ground,

And I will follow Emily's conjuring of a "swelling in the ground,"
and eternity will melt away hours, days, and years,
all voices will vanish in dreams of this time,
I could ask my children if they will remember this moment,
but they are already sleeping in the car, their breaths the only remaining sign,
and I turn on the headlights driving us this last time in the dark.

I don't remember a particular time or the sound of our shoes over the ground,
Were they ever my children as I find more dark in each never-ending year?
Do I even remember that moment on Forrester Street, creating words into signs?

Owning Venice for Awhile

The smell of the water,
the view as we approach the stop,
after all the noise of Kennedy Airport, Heathrow,
crowds pushing to get on the airport train,
we step into silence, hearing the sounds of plates,
a metal spoon scraping a pot on the stove,
this is not our city, this is theirs for so many years.
We walk into this dream of seawater, stone, and history.
Our voices lower without suggestion or command,
we just know what we should sound like here.

"I wanted to protect you from the rising ocean,
I wanted to be there to hold you in my arms
when the wave appears."

We are leaving the desert this early morning,
this world is disappearing as I write this down
words on paper floating away from me,
swallowed before I have a chance to
gather in all the letters of each word.

This is not the first time I have walked through water;
the patio is there with all the familiar cracks and the rain
goes on forever, gray after gray,
wet picnic bench and table
that sits there, uncovered,
confronting the storm,
only the fig tree in the back is nestled in for winter.
I smell the wood of the old windows,
feel the damp splinters under my fingers,
breath on glass, old pants above my ankles,
all I see is the wet grass, weeds growing

in cracks of the sidewalk,
I shiver as I lean into the hissing radiator
imagining a world that is not so flat
with my little girl hope.

I have not yet been to Venice,
but born from water, worked over garden soil,
smell of sour begonias, skin never really dry,
seagulls circling overhead looking for trash,
it is leading me there, leading me away.

Walking into the Mouth

> "You have to dig deep to bury Holy Mother."
>
> CLARISSA PINKOLA ESTÉS

Last night we wanted to walk into the cave of the mother
and dance like fools holding bones in our hands,
but all we had were sirens in Albuquerque
 and drunk shouting in the middle of the night.
My son winked at me once and said, "Don't forget your shoes,"
in another dream he talked to me while eating an orange
and I thought those pregnancy dreams meant something,
but I only got as far as being the fool walking on the mesa edge
and then what?

I call back to my grandmothers, my godmother
to remember the prayer my mother refused to teach me,
but I have traveled for too long,
I don't know if they can find me these days
as I sit in the eye socket of this one time ocean.
There are days I try not to create another disease,
who needs more of that in this world?
I move from washing dishes to sweeping dust balls,
and try to forget what it felt like looking out to
nothing but snow
 white on white and me crawling across it,
forgetting the boundaries of who I was.
Like I try to forget what it felt like waiting in the car
in a parking lot for the wave and knowing
there is nowhere to go.

I want to tell them I am here, and I am waiting to hear
the story of how they sit in the hand of God these days
and that we are all dancing in this connection,

one dance, as we move towards the cave, whistling
and clapping hands until we disappear into dark silence,
or perhaps it would go like this,
imagine this one as we feed on the desert spirits
outside of Albuquerque street lights,
and I realize I have always been swimming
across island, prairie, desert,
the women rub their rough hands over my forehead
and speak of crossings and ships and children with fevers,
they would find a horizon in a candle-lit bedroom
or see it in the oil they dropped in the water,
they speak of losing husbands, sisters, their own names,
they speak to me in my mother tongue,
no longer words but what has been seeping in my bones,
and I finally have something to say to them:
I talk of holding their tears under my skin
and walking over volcanoes, canyons and dark mesas,
holding their skeletons in my arms,
I will wake in a few days breathing in water.

Seven Mothers

"...the Matrikas are described as having inauspicious
qualities and often described as dangerous. They come to
play a protective role in later mythology, although some of
their inauspicious and wild characteristics still persist in these
accounts. Thus, they represent the prodigiously fecund aspect of
nature as well as its destructive force aspects."

WIKIPEDIA

I needed the Seven Mothers, the *Sapta Matrikas*,
when I was first carried into the house,
when I first started crying.
They would have destroyed what had fossilized into bone,
the old blood turning to volcanic rock:
"the one who is always right,"
"the one who wants what you have"
"the one who wants"
"the one who answers with a fist"
"the one who twists a story"
"the one who points a finger"
"the one who shares *malocchio*"
"the one who ignores all."

And my mother says again and again,
it has become a family nursery rhyme:
"you started to cry and you did not stop for months.
No one could get you to stop.
We did not know what was wrong."

If the Seven Mothers had been there,
they would have destroyed
all the ghosts trailing behind me,
ghosts of what was and what would be,

ghosts that would leave me
an orphan in a desert.

Using their weapons:
a fennel stalk, a serpent, silver coins,
a thunder bolt, volcanic ash, a noose,
spit, a sword, and a skull-bowl,
they walked the property,
hid under the small pile of rocks
near rotting vegetable plants,
hid in the corners of the "second garage,"
behind piles of newspapers and phone books,
curled in the chicken coop,
only speaking in dreams to each other,
slept under the house, breathing,
waiting for the moment.

Surround my crib so I won't
choke or burn with fever;
I call you to battle:
the boar-head mother,
the woman-lion mother.

But that never happened;
I did not know how to call out
to the Seven Mothers.
I did not know their language
as I walked around Long Island
in my polyester pants waiting
for something to happen.

I prayed to the tree at the end of the driveway,
and I made weapons from cereal boxes and glitter;
I left poems on pillows before I made my exit,
glue stuck on my fingers and all of you laughed.
I was the youngest, what did I know?

I know now the Seven Mothers
would want a sacrifice
for every word I learned,
and it would not have
ended with blood.

Grace

" . . . she is the muck that makes ideas happen."

CLARISSA PINKOLA ESTÉS

A hunchbacked woman carries a pail of water to her house
and a naked child walks toward the donkey
kicking a dust cloud into the eyes of the man
across from me coughing and looking at his watch.
I have been smelling my grandmother on my body these days
as I try to sleep, to eat,
I taste her walking down the hall,
the sound of her bedroom door
and I understand now
all that she was, without speaking a word.

In my darkened room,
the eyes tell stories instead of dreams,
singing instead of words and I am smoothing myself down
using tears and a waxing moon as my tools,
changing the story again,
and I will reflect hard enough and find
the deserted, empty public pool by the highway as
we drove by it every Sunday
on the way to my grandmother's house,
what happened to that pool again
after twenty years,
and I feel the weight of the china closet key in my hand
and she is winking, telling me to go on
and take another cookie,
"Go on," she whispers in Italian and the kitchen light burns
a hole through the center of my body,
and I dig deeper into the soil,
what is my grave, what is my food.

I will leave now and birth my own familiar house,
where the bones and skin are all my own smells, my own tongue,
where the turtle in the backyard
carries the heat of the day on her back
without using language,
and I never say a word to the tree of thorns,
I only bow and respect, and bury gifts of this world
out of fear and desire.

I will hold one foot in the ocean and the other on the mesa,
and I do not miss the ocean because
I am living in a prehistoric sea;
there are only ghosts of shells embedded in rock
and I am hardening into a fossil day by night,
finding ghosts of myself in the laundry room or the cellar.
You will not find me groping for the perfect word anymore,
the easy joke, the pleasure house of existing, of having fun---
it all fossilized during the last Great Drought;
I am finally the Mother of the Dead calling out to you,
reminding you of your own ultimate test,
I do not seek for what I have already lost,
I have lost most of my tongue,
I have lost some of my children,
I cannot remember my dreams.
I will not answer the phone because
desire disappeared along with my last laugh
and last warning in the muck.
Falling in love is a ritual I vaguely remember
my mother teaching me,
along with the command, "Don't lose your lunch money."

I walk by a man stretched on the street,
blood under his head,
and I whisper my blessing, "Grace."
I am the mother dolphin swimming past the coffin-builders
who mold aluminum, wood, velvet coffins all day and then
go home to a warm supper,

and there is all the land I want in this undiscovered country.
I am not a prisoner of your boundaries anymore,
waking in my dream, breathing,
holding the worms between my fingers in prayer.

After Kissing Anne Sexton's Lips

"My dark girls sing for this ..."
ANNE SEXTON, "LETTER WRITTEN ON A FERRY
WHILE CROSSING LONG ISLAND SOUND"

Anne sits in my porch, smoking,
pulling on her sweater,
she wants to tell me about the fairy tale,
the one where she is sleeping with me,
"How many abortions?" I ask.

We cross the Long Island Sound together,
"Oh, Anne, you talk of your husband
and I can barely see mine," I cry out.
She is wandering in that New England forest
and I have been in the desert for forty years.
Neither one of us talks to a priest
as we look at the blood in the toilet.

"Tell me about smoking in the bars" I beg,
and then maybe she will go on about
writing another letter of confession
to a doctor, a father, a god.
"It has to be a man," she dictates,
and I shape an O with my mouth
while I smoke.

We really do not understand each other.

I hope to find a river
to be baptized in all this dust
while the rosary tangles up around my ankles.
And she, well, she unbuttons my shirt and says,

"Let me tell you a secret,
imagination is only
the mouth of the mother.
Enter at your own risk."

But Anne, this is not a poem about risk,
this is a poem about the aftershock, the afterbirth,
what is left to examine.

Tarot and an Italian American Girl on Long Island

"Will I have children?"
"No."
"Are you sure?"
"That is not what the cards say."
"You don't know what you're talking about."
And maybe I didn't,
at 15 years old, what did I know?
Sitting on that polyester rug
in the living-room,
just another sweaty summer day,
and there was nothing else to do.
Days of looking at cards,
sitting too close to a fan,
killing a spider on the wall that just crawled out of nowhere,
why was I counting the days until summer when we ended up,
skin stuck to that worn out chair,
reading a magazine or a book,
was that when I was listening to
Carole King?
"Will you still love me tomorrow?"
There was no one there anyway,
only another day of cards.

Years later, I sit in my kitchen
and he says, "Put those cards away
before you hurt someone."
Too late for that.
Five of Cups,
that's me standing over those
cups on the ground, spilled blood,
and I don't see what is behind me,

the two cups there,
possibly waiting to offer me a way out.

But I had to find my own way out
and it wasn't going to be pretty.
The silence on our street often felt
like a choking, just hearing the noise of the fan or the television.
My mother watching her afternoon shows,
hours going by, day in and day out.
Then it was time for her to make
some dinner, and that meant calling me in, my sister in,
"Do the dishes" or
"Wash the salad."
Sleepy, almost in a dream state,
"What's wrong with you?"

"She doesn't know what she is doing.
She told me I won't have any kids."
What did I know?
I was looking in a book for the meanings of the cards,
but she was my future sister-in-law's sister and I had to be nice.
They laughed at me and started whispering,
what did she know, anyway.

I brought the cards to my friend,
living in New Jersey,
house, husband, children,
years after we ran around
Deer Park High School,
creating our secret language in the basement,
listening to "Bennie and the Jets" again and again.
no one cared about us, no one looked at us,
and then later she talked to me about leaving Deer Park,
going to the city to love a guy who claimed he was a warlock,
who claimed he would steal her soul away
and she only waited him to take more,
until it was time for that New Jersey house,

and the Nine of Pentacles appears;
the lady in her robe, one hand gentle on a pentacle,
the other a place for her bird,
it is all hers now:
the castle, the garden, the ground she stands on,
"Why do I get that card?
Why don't I get a card about spirituality
or selfless love?
 Why this?"

I took my spilled cups
and stopped talking.

I had to create myself,
whatever I was doing,
trying to write a song,
trying to start a band,
I did not want to go to college,
but I did.
Everyone around me wanted to be safe,
so we made our safe choices,
growing old at 17 years old.
This one is going to be a banker,
this one a diplomat,
this one an English teacher,
It was time to get serious.

And that was when I lost it,
the boy everyone believed I would marry,
the plan to move to New York
and become an actress,
I sat in my quiet small office,
studying literature,
losing it all.

Now I wander in this desert,
an old woman now,

the safe choices have moved in,
following me around for years,
the cards piled in boxes,

I begin to open them all
as if I am losing the skin
of all those years,
why did I get that card?
why me?

In the Long Island Sound with My Father

I remember holding on to my father's bumpy, cold neck
while he walked farther and farther out into the dark animal's belly.
We were past the point where the waves licked my legs.
"Come on, I'll take you far out," he said.
That was not what he usually said.
"Be careful," my mother's voice sang out from the blanket.
"There are rocks and animals that will bite."
That was what he usually said,
agreeing with my mother about animals biting
and strangers taking a rock and bashing you on the head.
He found my grandfather like that, on the ground,
bleeding, someone had bashed him on the head.

But that day, he was not afraid of the animals that might bite,
"I saw those animals when I came to this country,"
my mother's voice sang out again,
her black bathing-suit always looked new
because it never touched the ocean water.
She would only stand at the edge of water and sand
and stare out at the waves with a frown,
blaming that water for taking her to this place.
"Those animals are out there, somewhere," she said,
reminding me of what could happen:
a child strangled by an extension cord,
a brother dies from influenza,
an uncle falls from a donkey,
a husband is buried alive when a mine caves in,
a wife dies of breast cancer.

I started to slip and my father told me to "hold on."
I could see the seaweed underneath, taller than me.
It started to wrap around my legs,

whispering a name of someone we had forgotten,
someone we had lost . . .

"It's me . . . it's me."

Remembering What I Saw: A Glosa

> i was born with twelve fingers
> like my mother and my daughter.
> each of us
> born wearing strange black gloves
> extra baby fingers hanging over the sides of our cribs and
> dipping into milk.
>
> "LUCY AND HER GIRLS," LUCILLE CLIFTON

I arrive, an accident
crying day and night,
and of course there are too many eyes
and they are bleeding.
The diapers must go outside,
and I see the war,
but no one wants to look at me,
no one wants to talk to me,
no one wants to count the eyes.
I was born with twelve fingers
like my mother and my daughter.

My grandmother, who has an eye that twitches,
gives me the gold necklace,
gives it all to me:
the candles, the rosaries, the oil and water,
and the dead.
My hands start to knit:
one to pray and the other to curse.
each of us born wearing strange black gloves.

When I move to the desert
an invisible tongue appears,
and I use the language to carry

the bones of the living and the dead
to the volcano,
walk on the edge of its mouth,
words create the memory and the vision,
I no longer need to see,
all of the signs were there when I was born,
when I sat up in my crib, looking at the world,
and blinding the ones who cursed me,
extra baby fingers hanging over the sides of our cribs and
dipping into milk.

Language In My Mouth

"I want to thank my parents for placing the Navajo
language in my mouth."
EVANGELINE PARSONS YAZZIE, AT A READING IN GALLUP, NM

My parents with the rough smell of
grease or laundry detergent,
placed language in my mouth;
a twisted kind of language,
Napolitana with an immigrant New York attitude,
English from working-class neighborhoods in
Westchester County.
My father brought some dialect from his mother
who never learned English,
and my mother who struggled with her tongue for years,
learning English, forgetting Italian,
and what did it matter?
My language never fit.
Two children later and they don't understand me
most of the time,
don't know what I am talking about,
have no idea how my brain works or
what words float through my dreams.

It would be nice if my language was pure,
white as a young girl walking through an English garden,
easy straight lines from one generation to another,
like being George Eliot's grand-niece,
staring at portraits of a great-great-grandfather
who just stood there after a hunt.
But my language comes from tangled seaweed
wrapped around my ankles as I stand
in the used up water of the Long Island Sound,

now a survivor of the burning desert,
walking into the open mouth of the water
waiting for all the lines to simply disappear,
like the woman floating in the ocean only
desiring silence,
no one can speak to me anymore in my language,
not the way I remember it.

Once my language was shoved in my mouth,
that rough gift,
that mark on my forehead,
writing poetry was the wrong direction for me,
I should have known that years ago
before sitting in college classes, mute,
listening to the words fall out of
their mouths like music I could cry to,
but never create,
not with this rough tongue.

My parents used words for
what happened,
what was going to happen,
and what might happen.
Is that all of it?

Placing a language in someone's mouth
is quite a responsibility,
and no one wants to take ownership of that.
We drive by the cemetery and ignore the graves,
we do not want to see who is sitting beside us,
we do not want to hear any voices.
I take my daughter to the cemetery
and as we drive there the trees make me
feel I cannot breathe,
my daughter asks me why are we here
and why am I yelling at her
and why do I look like I can't breathe.

Seagulls eating through our trash,
the air is too wet and the woods
will not offer any bodies today,
as we sit in front of that almost dead ocean,
like a dream of blacks and blues
and the wave in front of us rises.

CARMELA DELIA LANZA grew up on Long Island, NY, in a working-class, Italian immigrant family. Her mother tongue was *Napoletana*. Eventually she learned English, and she spent a lot of time sitting in classrooms, not speaking. At home she tried to talk, but there were too many people around, doing most of the talking, so she spent a lot of time sitting on radiators and listening. She also spent a lot of time reading and writing. After years and years of living near the Atlantic Ocean, she moved to New Mexico and struggled to make a place for herself in the world. The spirits followed her, and she is grateful for that. Somewhere between the spine of the volcano and the ocean's womb, she finds her way in poetry.

Her writing has appeared in numerous journals and anthologies including *Ovunque Siamo*, *Comparative Woman*, *BorderSenses*, *Chantwood Magazine*, and *Voices in Italian Americana*. Her first chapbook of poetry, *Long Island Girl*, was published by Malafemmina Press. Finishing Line Press published her second chapbook of poetry, *So Rough A Messenger*. She is currently an associate professor of English at the University of New Mexico-Gallup branch, in Gallup, New Mexico.

www.ingramcontent.com/pod-product-compliance
Lightning Source LLC
Chambersburg PA
CBHW031141090426
42738CB00008B/1174